They laid him in a manger

They laid him in a manger

*A way to
the heart
of
Christmas*

New City
London   Dublin   Edinburgh

Texts from the German first published in *Zum Geburtstag des Herrn*
1987 © Verlag Neue Stadt

Translations from the German by *David Smith*

First published in Great Britain 1990,
Second edition 1993
by New City
57 Twyford Avenue, London W3 9PZ

British Cataloguing in Publication Data
    A catalogue record for this book
    is available from the British Library

    ISBN 0-904287-34-3

Typeset in Great Britain by Phoenix Typesetting,
Ilkley, West Yorkshire.

Printed in Great Britain by The Cromwell Press,
Broughton Grifford, Wiltshire.

Foreword

Christmas! Angels, the crib and carol singing! Peace
and good will! Surely that is the first thing which
comes to mind when we hear the word Christmas.
But what we in fact experience at Christmas is often
very different from such an idyllic image. The reality
is so often painful loneliness or a sharpening of
family quarrels. We become tense. It is a time when
peace is not in our homes. Even sending Christmas
cards and buying presents frequently becomes an
irritating burden.

So should we do away with Christmas? Or, if
we can't, just ignore it and go away on holiday -
if possible to somewhere where there is no trace
of Christmas? We ought surely to try to get away
from the shadow that is haunting us. After all, if we
are honest, we would all confess to having certain
expectations at Christmas time. In our hearts, we
hope to meet others we do not otherwise see or to
be surprised by an unexpected greeting and we look
forward to receiving presents as a sign of love. We
want our families to be united and at peace and we
long at Christmas for the innocence and trust that we

5

had in our relationship with our parents when we were children. It is a time when we all want to be accepted and feel secure.

No, it is just not possible to get away from this longing in our hearts. It won't be silenced. The mere fact that we are so frequently saddened by the thought of yet another Christmas and are sceptical about the success of the celebration is proof of the power of this longing.

Christmas, then, is often not what it should be for us. We have high expectations of it that are not fulfilled and this makes us feel very lonely. We are conscious too of the distress and suffering of people in so many parts of our world. But that is precisely the state of darkness in which Christmas should take place! The star of Bethlehem does not shine in the bright lights of the shop windows and the Christmas message cannot be heard in hi-fi carol singing.

Christmas is really a very gentle and quiet time. It is not at all romantic. It is not a fulfilment or a successful conclusion. It is no more than a beginning. It is the shining of a little light in a great darkness. If we have darkness in us, if we are conscious of distress and need around us, then Christmas has a message for us. We must not try to avoid it, but must be aware that we can open our hands at Christmas time to the gift that God wants to make to us. We can be 'straw', it may be night and we may have no home, but in this way hope can be born.

That is how it was at the first Christmas and that is how it can be at every Christmas. In the crib new life begins. In the night a star shines. In the stall a child is born.

It may be very difficult to speak about Christmas, but perhaps this is because it is an event without parallel in history. Christmas is not an idea. It is not a theology. It is a child – a defenceless, homeless child. Christmas is so small that there is no one who cannot receive this little child. There was simply a mother and a carpenter and shepherds . . .

Jesus came not because we are so good, but because he is so good. Anyone who is able to believe that can experience something of Christmas. If Christ had only been born in Bethlehem and not in our hearts, then we would never have known how much we are loved.

When people think about what Christmas means for them, they are usually able to speak about childhood experiences, some of them good, but others bitter. What Christmas has meant to those in whose hearts Christ has been born again will be found in the texts that appear in the pages that follow.

Wilfried Hagemann

In the beginning was the Word
and the Word was with God
and the Word was God.
He was in the beginning with God;
all things were made through him,
and without him was not anything made
that was made.
In him was life
and the life was the light of men.
The light shines in the darkness
and the darkness has not overcome it.
The true light
that enlightens every man
was coming into the world.
He was in the world
and the world was made through him,
yet the world knew him not.
He came into his own home
and his own people received him not.
But to all who received him,
he gave power to become children of God;
to all who believed in his name,
who were born not of blood,
nor of the will of the flesh,
nor of the will of man,
but of God.
And the Word became flesh
and dwelt among us.
We have beheld his glory,

glory as of the only Son of the Father,
full of grace and truth.

John 1:1-5, 9-14

The drama of human freedom is at the
heart of the Prologue to John's Gospel. It
is concerned with us, our everyday life and
the decisions which we, in our freedom,
are called to make. Christmas confronts us
with the unlimited possibility of salvation
that was revealed to us when the Word
of God entered our human history. What
Saint John is telling us is that this possibility
does not become a reality just of its own
accord. It is an offer made to us in our
freedom, something that we can either
reject or accept. Celebrating the feast of
Christmas means making room for the Lord
who is coming.

Carlo Maria Martini
(Archbishop of Milan, b.1927)

$\mathbf{A}$nd the Word became flesh
and dwelt among us.
God's Word became human
to accustom human beings
to receiving God.
God had begun
to live with the human race.

Irenaeus
(Bishop of Lyons,
Second Century)

With the fullness of time he appeared – the one who wanted to set us free from time. For, set free from time, we would be able to reach that eternity which is beyond time. We would therefore no longer need to say: When will the hour come? For it would be an eternal day. No yesterday would precede it and no tomorrow would follow it.

In this world, however, days go by and others come. No day remains. Even as we speak, the moments pass, the first syllable pressed on by the second that is waiting impatiently to be heard. As soon as we have spoken, we have become a little older. I am certainly older now than I was this morning. Nothing stands still. Nothing remains firm in time. We must therefore love the one through whom the times came to be, so that we may be set free from time and become established in eternity, where time and the changes it brings no longer exist.

It is, then, a great mercy on the part of our Lord Jesus Christ that he, through whom the times came to be, came to be for our sakes in time, that he, through whom all things came to be, came to be in the midst of all things, that he became what he had made. For he became what he had made. He, who had made the human race, became human, so that what he had made would not be lost.

Augustine
(Bishop of Hippo, d. 430)

The Word became flesh.
The Word became heart.
God accepted a heart.
God's heart beats
in the countless millions
of human hearts.
Since then
we are able to know
what dwells in the heart of humanity,
because God who knows everything
wanted to be close to everything.
Not only did he want to know
what is in the heart of humanity –
he also wanted to experience it.
What is in our heart
may be troubled and disturbed,
but there is in it
always a longing
for the answer 'yes' –
'Don't write me off!' –
'Forgive me!' –
'Give me another chance!' –
'Accept me!' 'Do you love me?'
And there is even more than this
in every heart –
an even deeper mystery.
It is not just a longing –
it is reality.
Every heart is a heart that is loved.

For every human heart
is worth God's own heart
and God has offered himself up
for every human being.

Klaus Hemmerle
(Bishop of Aachen)

In those days a decree went out from
Caesar Augustus that all the world should
be enrolled. This was the first enrolment,
when Quirinius was governor of Syria.
And all went to be enrolled, each to his own
city.

And Joseph also went up from Galilee, from
the city of Nazareth, to Judea, to the city of
David, which is called Bethlehem, because
he was of the house and lineage of David, to
be enrolled with Mary, his betrothed, who
was with child.

And while they were there, the time
came for her to be delivered. And she gave
birth to her first-born son and wrapped
him in swaddling cloths and laid him in
a manger, because there was no place for
them in the inn.

And in that region there were shepherds
out in the field, keeping watch over their
flock by night. And an angel of the Lord
appeared to them and the glory of the Lord
shone around them and they were filled
with fear. And the angel said to them,
'Do not be afraid, for behold, I bring you
good news of great joy which will come
to all the people, for to you is born this
day in the city of David a Saviour, who is

18

Christ the Lord. And this will be a sign for you:

'You will find a babe wrapped in swaddling cloths and lying in a manger.'

And suddenly there was with the angel a multitude of the heavenly host praising God and saying:

'Glory be to God in the highest,
and on earth peace,
good will among men.'

When the angels went away from them into heaven, the shepherds said to one another, 'Let us go over to Bethlehem and see this thing that has happened, which the Lord has made known to us.' And they went with haste and found Mary and Joseph and the babe lying in a manger.

And when they saw it, they made known the saying which had been told them concerning this child. And all who heard it wondered at what the shepherds told them. But Mary kept all these things, pondering them in her heart.

And the shepherds returned, glorifying and praising God for all they had heard and seen, as it had been told them.

Luke 2: 1-20

He became a child
so that you could become a full mature human
   being.
He was wrapped in swaddling cloths
so that you could be unravelled
from the meshes of death.
He came on earth
so that you could live beneath the stars.
There was no place for him in the inn
so that there could be many dwelling places
for you in heaven.
He was rich,
but he became poor for us.
His poverty is our riches
and his weakness is our strength.
He is poor for us,
but in himself he is rich.
You can see him
lying there in swaddling cloths,
but what you cannot see
is that he is God's Son.

Ambrose
(Bishop of Milan, d. 397)

Jesus came into this world, but he did not tell anyone, even those who were closest to him, who he was. If he had entered the world in his home in Nazareth, his coming might have been celebrated with great rejoicing by all his relatives and by the neighbours and all those who lived in the town. But he was born on a journey and in the midst of a great number of unknown people. So he really does belong to everyone – and he came very reticently, making no noise. There is no doubt God might have been able to do much more to spread the news of his coming, but it is clear that he does not want to thrust his Son upon us. He wants us to come to him. We have to look for him. We have to discover him. Yes, Jesus is infinitely reticent. He waits.

All the historical events surrounding Jesus' birth in Bethlehem at the turn of the age proclaim God in the silence of words. They were prophetic events speaking in silence to all the generations that have followed. But they are not in any way insistent, demanding to be understood at once. Jesus is patient. He has time.

René Voillaume
(Founder of the Little Brothers of Jesus)

Thys endris nyghth
I saw a syghth,
A stare as bryght as day,
And ever among
A mayden song,
"Lullay, by, by, lullay."

That lovely lady sat and song,
And to hyr chyld sayd,
"My Sone, my Broder, my Fader der,
Why lyest thou thus in haye?
My swete byrd,
Thus it ys betyde,
Thow thou be kyng veray,
But nevertheles
I wyll not ses
To syng, "By, by, lullay."

The chyld than spak in hys talkyng,
And to hys moder sayd,
"I be kyndde ame kyng,
In crybbe thou I be layd.
For aungelles bryght
Done to me lyght,
Thou knowest it ys no nay;
And of that syght
Thou mayst be lyght
To syng, 'By, by, lullay'."

thys endris: this other   *veray:* truly   *ses:* cease

22

"Now, swet Son, syn thou art kyng,
Why art thou layd in stall?
Why ne thou ordende thi beddyng
In sum gret kynges hall?
Me thynkyth it is ryght
That kyng or knyght
Shuld ly in good aray,
And than among
It wer no wrong
To syng, 'By, by, lullay'."

"Mary moder, I am thi chyld
Thow I be layd in stall;
Lordes and dukes shal worsshyp me,
And so shall kynges all.
Ye shall well se
That kynges thre
Shal come the Twelfe Day.
For this behest
Yefe me thi brest
And syng, 'By, by, lullay'."

"Now tell me, swet Son, I the pray,
Thou art me leve and dere,
How shuld I kepe the to thi pay
And mak the glad of chere?
For all thi wyll
I wold fullfyll,
Thou wotyste full well in fay,
And for all this
I wyll the kys
And syng, 'By, by, lullay'."

23

"My der moder, whan tym it be,
Thou take me up on loft,
And set me upon thi kne,
And handyll me full soft,
And in thi arme
Thou hyl me warme,
And kepe nyght and day;
If I wepe
And may not slepe,
Then syng, 'By, by, lullay'."

"Now, swet Son, syn it is so,
That all thyng is at thi wyll,
I pray the, graunte me a bone
Yf it be both ryght and skyll:
That chyld or man
That wyl or kan
Be mery upon my day,
To blyse hem bryng,
And I shal syng,
'Lullay, by by, lullay'."

An ancient carol

hyl: cover

This day to you a child is born
of maiden, chosen from all time.
A child so tender and so fine
should be your joy this Christmas morn.

He's Christ our Lord, our God who reigns.
He longs to save us from our woe,
his saving task to undergo
and wash us clean from sin and stain.

Praise be to God enthroned on high,
who sends his own beloved Son,
while angels sing in unison –
'a glad New Year' their joyful cry.

He brings you all great happiness,
prepared by God our Father's love,
that we with him in heaven above
may live in everlasting bliss.

Ah Lord, who madest all from clay,
how couldst thou be so small and poor,
to lie there in the dusty straw
where ox and ass feed every day?

Martin Luther
(1483–1546)

I sing the birth was born to-night,
The author both of life and light;
　　The angels so did sound it,
And, like the ravished shepherds said,
Who saw the light, and were afraid,
　　Yet searched, and true they found it.

The Son of God, the eternal king,
That did us all salvation bring,
　　And freed our soul from danger,
He whom the whole world could not take,
The Word, which heaven and earth did make,
　　Was now.laid in a manger.

The Father's wisdom willed it so,
The Son's obedience knew no 'No';
　　Both wills were in one stature,
And, as that wisdom had decreed,
The Word was now made flesh indeed,
　　And took on Him our nature.

What comfort by Him we do win,
Who made Himself the price of sin,
　　To make us heirs of glory!
To see this babe, all innocence,
A martyr born in our defence,
　　Can man forget the story?

Ben Jonson
(1572–1637)

26

This day our Father did create
may all the world commemorate!
Praise for what Jesus Christ his Son
in heaven and on earth has done!

Long have the nations waited you
until God's promised time was due.
Then from his throne he sent you down
to save the world – his own dear Son.

When I attempt with all my skill
to grasp this thought, my mind is still
and contemplates, as it adores,
the endless love that God outpours.

Rejoice, you heavens, that on earth
is brought this day a holy birth
and earth, that sees him born today,
sing a new anthem while you may!

This day our Father did create
may all the world commemorate!
Praise for what Jesus Christ his Son
in heaven and on earth has done!

Christian Fürchtegott Gellert
(1715–1769)

I stand here by your manger bed,
O Jesus, life to me!
I bring no gift but what instead
you gave me lovingly.
Take it – it is my mind and soul,
my heart, my spirit, courage, all!
And may it give you pleasure.

For long before I came to be,
you came with saving grace
to choose me from eternity
before I knew your face.
Even before your moulding hand
had fashioned me, your love had planned
how you would shape my future.

I look at you with heartfelt joy
and cannot gaze my fill.
I know no better way to employ
my time than standing still.
O that my mind were an abyss,
my soul an ocean fathomless –
that I might comprehend you!

Paul Gerhardt
(1607–1676)

Lord! when thou didst thy selfe undresse
Laying by thy robes of glory,
To make us more, thou wouldst be lesse,
And becam'st a wofull story.

To put on Clouds instead of light,
And cloath the morning-starre with dust,
Was a translation of such height
As, but in thee, was ne'r exprest;

Brave wormes, and Earth! that thus could have
A God Enclos'd within your Cell,
Your maker pent up in a grave,
Life lockt in death, heav'n in a shell;

Ah, my deare Lord! what couldst thou spye
In this impure, rebellious clay,
That made thee thus resolve to dye
For those that kill thee every day?

O what strange wonders could thee move
To slight thy precious bloud, and breath!
Sure it was *Love*, my Lord; for *Love*
Is only stronger far than death.

Henry Vaughan
(c. 1621–1695)

The Lord has sent me
to bring good news to the poor.
Christmas is the feast of the poor –
a very poor feast,
the birth of a child
who was rejected by everyone.
And the first to come to the crib
were simple people –
shepherds, poor people.
They were the first
to hear the good news
and to be told:
'Today the Saviour is born for you.'

Jean Vanier
(Founder of the Arche
Centres for the Handicapped,
b. 1929)

How I admire the Lord,
the Creator of the world!
He wanted to be born
not surrounded by gold and silver,
but just on a piece of this earth.

Saint Jerome
(Latin Church Father, d. 420)

You are with us, Emmanuel.
You are with us as a human being,
as a new-born child,
weak and vulnerable,
wrapped in swaddling cloths
and lying in a crib
'because there was no place for them at the inn'.
Could you ever have done any more
than you did
to be our Emmanuel, God with us?

Pope John Paul II
(b.1920)

Jesus,
what made you so small?
Love!

Bernard of Clairvaux
(1090–1153)

★★★

Since this holy night
God has been in this world
and the world has been in God.

Odo Casel
(1886–1948)

This is the month, and this the happy morn
Wherein the Son of Heav'n's eternal King,
Of wedded maid, and virgin mother born,
Our great redemption from above did bring;
For so the holy sages once did sing,
    That he our deadly forfeit should release,
And with his Father work us a perpetual peace.

That glorious form, that light unsufferable,
And that far-beaming blaze of majesty,
Wherewith he wont at Heav'n's high
        council-table
To sit the midst of Trinal Unity,
He laid aside; and here with us to be,
    Forsook the courts of everlasting day,
And chose with us a darksome house of mortal
                                clay.

Say Heav'nly Muse, shall not thy sacred vein
Afford a present to the Infant God?
Hast thou no verse, no hymn, or solemn strain,
To welcome him to this his new abode,
Now while the heav'n by the sun's team untrod,
    Hath took no print of the approaching light,
And all the spangled host keep watch in
                        squadrons bright?

See how from far upon the eastern road
The star-led Wisards haste with odours sweet,
O run, prevent them with thy humble ode,
And lay it lowly at his blessed feet;
Have thou the honour first, thy Lord to greet,
    And join thy voice unto the angel quire,
From out his secret altar toucht with hallow'd
                                    fire.

John Milton
(1608–1674)

When the King of Kings was born,
he chose his parents
from among the little people of this world.
And the simple people of the district
were the first he invited to his cradle –
those who slept under the stars of heaven
and could hear the angel's voice.
It was only then
that he received the great ones of the world.
They were also his children,
but their lives were threatened
by glory and honour.
He called them,
but they were so far off
that the journey took them a long time.
Those mighty kings announced their arrival
with expensive presents.
But first they kneeled down –
humility was their real gift.
They kneeled down
after the shepherds.
That is how Christmas was
and that is how it will be
until the end of the world.

Gilbert Cesbron
(French author, b. 1913)

A light has come from Bethlehem
that has continued to enlighten
the hearts of men and women.
The angels' message
again and again gives us new hope.
Centuries have passed since then
and so much has happened
to make us lose heart –
wars and disasters
and disappointments of every kind.
But that good news,
the grace of that child
and the happiness of that mother
have continued to help people and nations
to free themselves from the night
in which they again and again
have found themselves straying.

Igino Giordani
(Italian author, 1894–1980)

God became a child
in order to tell us
that he is not far away.
The angels are singing:
'Peace to people on earth.'
We ask him,
who became defenceless
because he was powerless,
that he will extinguish in us
the flame of the pride of power
and take hatred out of our hearts,
filling them with love,
so that it will not be long
before no nation in the world
will remember what war is.

Chiara Lubich (b.1920)

While gentle silence enveloped all things,
and night in its swift course was now half
gone,
thy all-powerful word leaped from heaven,
from the royal throne,
into the midst of the land
that was doomed,
a stern warrior,
carrying the sharp sword
of thy authentic command.

Wis. 18:14–16a

Were my eyes to see you come down,
they would cease to weep.
Rain him down, you clouds –
the one whom earth has longed for.

Earth, you have given us only thorns.
Be open now and bring forth
the only flower
in which you yourself may flourish.

John of the Cross
(1542–1591)

H ow much you have loved us,
kind Father!
If your Word had not become flesh
and had not dwelt among us,
we would have had to believe
that there was no connection
between God and humanity
and we would have been in despair.

Augustine
(Bishop of Hippo,
d. 430)

With Jesus a new humanity was born, consisting of heaven and earth, of the visible and the invisible and of human and divine hope. It is composed of members who are citizens both of heaven and of earth, human children and children of God. In his power, every human being can be the son or daughter of the most high God and the dwelling place of God on earth and every man and woman can inherit heaven.

The Word became flesh. God became human and human beings were able to look at God on this earth. If Jesus is really God who became human, then something is bound to have changed fundamentally in human history. If God really entered our history, then that history must have been placed under a new sign.

When God became human, humanity became 'God's space' and men and women became related to God and Christ's brothers and sisters. If God became one of us in Jesus, that is surely something that we can never value highly enough. We can place all our human hopes on him. If Jesus is at the same time both God and our brother, then I should never know fear again.

God is my brother. This reveals new horizons to us and changes our whole existence. Our measures have changed – the kingdom of God is above all immeasurable. We inherit God. With all our sins, we are saints!

Carlo Carretto
(1910–1988)

The one who embraces everything
and who created everything
came into the world
like every other person!
We hear the one at whose word
the angels and archangels tremble
cry like a child.
He did not need to become human,
because we humans were created by him,
but we needed
God to become flesh
and dwell among us.
His lowliness is our distinction
and his ignominy is our honour.
What he continues to be,
by becoming flesh as God,
we become,
renewed from the flesh into God.

Hilary
(Bishop of Poitiers, d. 367)

Christmas, a season of paradox, when the topsy-turvy logic of the divine becomes most evident: the Infinite shut in the finite, the Almighty reduced to a powerless babe, the Light and Life of All Ages bursting into history in the dark dead of winter.

Is this not the work of love – love which seeks always to become the other, and in becoming that which is other than itself affirms itself as love? Is it not a prefiguring of the climax of love on this earth, in the death of Jesus on the cross when love became nothing, taking non-love on itself and becoming sin? Christmas and the paschal mystery both shout out that love in losing itself is itself, utterly itself.

And both moments show us the pathway of love, the secret of God's own inner life which we all can share.

Charles Wheatley
(b.1955)

God's becoming human
is not an idyll.
It is a scandal!
God meets us
in the lowliness of a child.

Klaus Hemmerle
(Bishop of Aachen)

When the time had come
that God had previously chosen
for the redemption of humankind,
his Son, Jesus Christ
lodged on our lowly earth.
He, the incomprehensible one,
wanted to be grasped.
He who was before all time
took his beginning in time.
He who was invisible in his being
became visible in our flesh.
The God who was incapable of suffering
was not ashamed to be
a human being capable of suffering.
The God who was immortal
submitted himself to the law of death.

Leo the Great
(Pope, d. 461)

If we are to understand what happened at Bethlehem, we need God's revelation. It is not possible to know just from the child in the crib that the Son of God is concealed in him. He appears, after all, incognito. This tension is present at the centre of the mystery of Christmas. Majesty assumes the form of lowliness, strength appears as weakness and eternity is presented as mortality. God comes to us very quietly. He does not herald his power with a trumpet blast. Golgotha is already secretly proclaimed in the babe lying in the manger.

God becomes one of us. He takes on himself the frailty of human life. It is not just a case of interbreeding with humankind. God does not simply become a divine human hybrid. He remains entirely what he is – God from God – and becomes entirely human. He does not slip into the disguise or the mask of a single ready made person with a particular name. No, he assumes human 'nature' – the nature that we all have, even though we all have that nature in our own individual expression of it. That is why God's becoming human has something to do with the whole of humanity. God, who is infinitely holy, becomes a poor human servant. Deep abysses which cannot be bridged are spanned – heaven and earth, death and life, God and humankind, poverty and plenty, eternity and mortality. He becomes poor so that we may become rich.

Why, then, does God come to us incognito and under the sign of poverty? This has always puzzled men and women and made them reflect. As Pope Leo the Great said, 'the lowliness of God is for us much more wonderful than his power and it is much more difficult for us to understand his self-emptying of his divine majesty than his exaltation of himself from the form of a servant'. There is only one answer to this – God has mercy on us. His becoming human in Jesus Christ is the revelation of God's inexpressible sympathy for men and women. It is the great and everlasting sacrament of his great mercy.

Karl Lehmann
(Bishop of Mainz)

You wanted to be God,
although you were human
and so you were lost.
He wanted to be human,
although he was God,
so that he could look for what was lost.
Your human pride struck you down
with such force
that only the humility of God
could make you rise up again.

Augustine
(Bishop of Hippo, d. 430)

God's Son became human
so that human beings might have their home
in God.

Hildegard of Bingen
(1098–1179)

The one who has from eternity
been in the bosom of the Father
is now resting on his mother's knees.
God is so close to you
that he lets himself be embraced like a child
and held like a baby at the breast –
for 'the Word became flesh
and dwelt among us'.
How is it possible for him
to be more like you
and more closely related to you?
Look, he has your flesh and bones!
God has become your brother.

Thomas à Kempis
(1379/80–1471)

Jesus comes back into the world
when we offer him a dwelling-place in our
    hearts,
when we accept him in his law of love,
when we do what Mary did
and conceive Jesus and carry him in us,
so that he is able to become
the heart of our life.
Then he will love the heavenly Father
with our whole heart,
with our whole soul
and with all our strength.
Then his love and goodness
and his sympathy for all men and women
will shine out into the world
like a light through us.
Then he will smile through our eyes
and help with our hands
and once again live
his redeeming life of the Gospel.
Then we shall be the doors,
the tens and hundreds of thousands of doors,
through which he, the Lord, the Prince of Peace,
God-with-us, will enter
his world, his kingdom.

Werenfried van Straaten

The new world order is this –
God lets himself be so influenced
by his love for his image and likeness
that he becomes a little baby.
He lets himself be laid in a crib
to show that he will be
both shepherd and pasture
for his people.
He, who is eternity without ageing,
subjects himself to the human law
of becoming older.
Although he is God,
he takes all suffering onto himself
like a weak human being.
He does this
to put an end to the law of death
and to enable us to share in immortality.
God's power is this:
that he can be what he is not
and yet still remain what he is.
He is our God –
the eternal Son of the eternal Father.
He is God and he is human,
because he stands in the middle,
between the Father and us.
The reality of his flesh is revealed
in his weakness
and the reality of his majesty is revealed
in his miracles.

Zeno
(Bishop of Verona, d. 371/72)

God fulfilled the promises that he had made to his prophets and gave his people what they had been longing for, but everything turned out differently from what they had expected. God's thoughts are always quite different from human thoughts. They seem at first to fall short of our expectations, but in fact they go far beyond them – as far as heaven is from our earth.

God came on earth as a human being and first revealed his human love in the human face of a little child. He did not come in terrible majesty, in overwhelming light or in visible power and glory. He came in weakness and impotence. He almost came secretly. He was even despised and rejected. He did not come to display his omnipotence, to make wisdom shine on the world, to judge evil or to help justice to be victorious. That was not his way of establishing a kingdom of God on earth. No, he came to reveal God's *agape*, in other words, that self-giving, sacrificial love that is only present in God.

That is the sublime wisdom of the mystery of Christianity – that God is *agape* and that his *agape* shone on us in a human face, the face of the kindest, most selfless and most loving of all human beings.

Odo Casel
(1886–1948)

The birthday of the Lord
is the birthday of peace.

The birth of Christ
is the origin of the Christian people
and the birthday of the head
is also the birthday of the body.

Leo the Great
(Pope, d. 461)

Christmas.
Heaven has opened its gates.
The Word has become flesh
and has brought
the fire of love
to earth.

Because we do not want
this day ever to end,
we ask you, Lord,
that we may love one another
as you loved us
and we ask you
to stay among us,
present in our midst.

In that way every day
could be Christmas day for us.

Chiara Lubich
(b.1920)

Christmas!
On that night
was born in a manger the poor man
whose love was to shake the world.

Christmas!
Since that time no one has the right
to be happy in isolation.

Raoul Follereau
(1903–1977)

Anyone who has really understood
that God became human
can never speak and act
in an inhuman way.

Karl Barth
(1886–1968)

We are not just promised freedom –
we have it already.
It is not a present in the future –
it has been given to us.
It has not simply been predicted –
it is present here and now.
For with the fullness of time
came the fullness of God.

Where else does such great love exist?
Today we can understand
the depth of God's concern for us.
Today we can experience
what he thinks of us.

Bernard of Clairvaux
(1090–1153)

He is simply there –
that is all
that he does
or that he can do.
But, by being there,
powerless yet radiant,
it is God himself
who is there.
God is there for us.
What, then, does this being God
in the child of Bethlehem
say to us?
It says to me and to you
and to every human being:
It is good that you are there.

Klaus Hemmerle
(Bishop of Aachen)

What suitable response can we make
to such a great honour –
the honour that you have bestowed on us
by giving us such great love?
God's only Son,
whose divine origin
is beyond description,
entered the womb of the holy Virgin
and assumed the form of a human being.
He, who holds everything in being
and in whom and for whom everything exists,
was born in harmony
with the laws of human nature.
The one, at whose voice
angels and archangels tremble
and heaven and earth
and all the elements of this world melt away,
the unseen one,
who does not let himself
be confined to any human reality,
whom we can neither touch, nor feel, nor hold –
we see him in a crib,
wrapped in swaddling cloths.
Anyone who thinks about these things
that are so unworthy of God
will be all the more strongly
convinced of his love.
For him, by whose will we were created,
it was, after all, not necessary

to become human.
But it was for us
that he assumed human nature
and wanted to live among us.
His humility
is our great dignity.
God was born as a human being!
Or, to look at it
from another point of view,
we were reborn in God.

Hilary
(Bishop of Poitiers, d. 367)

This Body is not the Cloud, but a Pillar assumd to manifest His Lov unto us. In these Shades doth this Sun break forth most Oriently. In this Death is His Lov Painted in most lively colours. GOD never shewd Himself more a GOD, then when He appeared Man. Never gained more Glory then when He lost all Glory. Was never more Sensible of our Sad Estate, then when He was bereaved of all Sence.

Thomas Traherne
(1637–1674)

God is the Lord
and he appeared to us.
He came, not in the form of God,
so that he would not frighten the weak,
but in the form of a servant,
so that he could lead the enslaved to freedom.
Is there anyone
who is so weary
or so ungrateful
not to be overjoyed
at this day?

Basil the Great
(Bishop of Caesarea, d. 379)

Jesus Christ – God who became human, a child of poor people. Even as a baby at the breast he was on the run. He was treated with indifference and injustice and he often failed. He was spied on, betrayed, denounced and arrested by the High Priests. He was locked up in Jerusalem. We can talk easily today about that sort of thing – we have all the right words. He was put on trial. Anyone who has been in the dock would know what that means and find it amazing that Jesus Christ, who went through all that, was God.

Why did God become human? That is a question that has troubled many very clever people. Every possible kind of answer has been given, many of them very good, others less satisfactory. One of the greatest of those who looked for an answer was Augustine. He said: God became human so that we too might become human.

Are we not really human, then? Certainly we often live for ourselves, when we should be living for others. We brush past others, live alongside them without even a cold glance at them, when we should be living with them, our fellow human beings, as members of the same society, full of fellow feeling for them, suffering with them, ready to share and work with them and for them. We are often not human at all –

mean, inhuman, cruel, behaving like brutes.
We are sub-human, preferring to live in a dark
subterranean world where we can follow our
own evil ways. But we must become human –
all of us! And God became human to give us the
strength to become human in Christ.

Julius Angerhausen
(in an address to prisoners)

Jesus did not come exclusively
for people with white skins,
nor did he come only for black people.
He did not come simply for Europeans
or just for people in other parts of the world.
Christ became human
for the whole of humankind.
That means
he also came for each one of us.
It also means
a feast for all of us,
joy for all of us
and freedom and peace
for all of us.

Chiara Lubich
(b.1920)

Gold, friends, power and honour –
nothing can make us so happy
as the joyful news
that Christ became man.
The human heart can scarcely conceive it
and we can certainly not talk enough about it.
To do such a thing
and let us hear about it,
God must love us with all his heart.
He must love me
because he comes so close to me,
because he became human with me.
He became
what I am.

Martin Luther
(1483–1546)

God, the Lord, has made his mercy known –
his song has sounded in the night.

This is the day that the Lord has made –
let us be glad and rejoice in it!

The dear and holy child has been given to us
as our companion on the way.

He was born in a manger –
there was no place in the inn.

Glory to God in the highest
and peace on earth among people of good will!

May the heavens rejoice
and the earth shout with joy!
Let the sea exult
and all that it surrounds!
let the fields be glad
and all that grows in them!

Sing a new song to the Lord –
let every land sing to the Lord!

For the Lord is great and worthy of our
    praise,
greater than all other gods.

All nations, praise the Lord,
and all the people of the earth, praise him!
Honour the name of the Lord!

Francis of Assisi
(1181/2–1226)

God's Son became a human being.
All our efforts to understand
this great mystery are in vain.
All that we can do
is what the shepherds did –
worship, believe and praise God.

Cardinal Alfred Bengsch
(1921–1979)

The shepherds sing; and shall I silent be?
  My God, no hymn for Thee?
My soul's a shepherd too; a flock it feeds
  Of thoughts, and words, and deeds.
The pasture is Thy Word; the streams Thy
                                grace,
  Enriching all the place.
Shepherd and flock shall sing, and all my
                                powers
  Outsing the daylight hours;
Then we will chide the sun for letting night
  Take up his place and right;
We sing one common Lord; wherefore He
                                should
  Himself the candle hold.

George Herbert
(1593–1633)

Who could doubt the greatness of this event –
that the exalted ruler of the world should come
down from such a great distance to a place that was
so unworthy? Why, then, did he come down? We
know why, because what he actually said and did
tell us clearly the reason for his coming. He hurried
down from the mountains to look among the
hundreds of sheep for the one that had gone astray.
He came for our sake, so that his mercy and his
wonderful deeds would proclaim to the human race
even more visibly the praise of the Lord.

How wonderful is the condescension of the God
who seeks us and how great is the dignity of those
who are sought by him! All the wealth and all the
glory of the world and everything that is desirable in
the world – none of this means so much as this great
honour. Nothing can be compared with it. Lord,
what is the human race, that you have made it so
great? Why are you so attached to it?

It would have been more appropriate, surely, if
we had come to him. But two things prevented
us from doing that. Our eyes were clouded and he
dwells in inaccessible light. And we were crippled
and could not come to him. That is why he came to
us – he, the physician of our souls.

Bernard of Clairvaux
(1090–1153)

The middle of the night
is the beginning of the day.
The middle of need
is the beginning of the light.

From an old carol

The light that shines in the darkness
is in no sense abstract,
nor is it just ordinary.
It is not simply a demand imposed on us
to be good to each other.
No, it is something
that is both living and personal.
It is Jesus Christ,
Mary's son and the Son of God.
Mary was the first to understand
that her life had been given
an entirely new meaning
and that, in this child,
the life of the whole of humanity
had been made new.

Carlo Maria Martini
(Archbishop of Milan)

Praise to the holy Trinity,
who decided
that human dignity should be restored
and that the devil's cunning
should be put to shame.
I praise you, heavenly Father,
who sent your beloved Son
into this world
to redeem us.
I praise you,
Son of God, Jesus Christ,
who assumed our nature
in order to redeem us human beings.
I praise you, Comforter, Holy Spirit,
who, from the beginning to the end,
have wonderfully and gloriously carried out
all the saving acts of our redemption.
Praise, glory, honour and blessing
be yours, most exalted Trinity,
the origin and the beginning
of our feast today
and the source of our joy!

Thomas à Kempis
(1379/80–1471)

Christmas is our feast.

Today we celebrate God's coming to us so that we might return to him, taking off the old nature and putting on the new. As we died in Adam, so we shall live in Christ, by being born with him, crucified with him and rising again with him.

Be glad about his conception and leap, perhaps not like John the Baptist in his mother's womb, but certainly like David, when the ark of the covenant reached its resting place.

Honour the enrolment, by which you have been enrolled for heaven.

Celebrate the birth, by which you have been redeemed.

Respect little Bethlehem, which has brought you back to paradise.

Revere the crib, by which you were nourished by the Word, after having lost knowledge.

Follow the star and with the wise men offer gifts to him who died for you.

Praise him with the shepherds, sing joyful songs with the angels and dance with the archangels.

Together let us celebrate the feast in heaven and on earth, for I am certain that those who are in heaven are also rejoicing, because they love the God-man.

Gregory Nazianzen
(330–390)

The human race was made God's likeness,
but, since we lost that form,
God took our human likeness
this night, when he was born.

Andreas Gryphius
(1616–1664)

The night is near its ending,
the day is drawing near.
Our songs of praise ascending,
bright morning star, appear!
The man who suffers nightly
can share in others' joy.
The star that shines so brightly
will fear and pain destroy.

The angels serve, revering
this child, a servant now,
for God himself appearing
atones for broken law.
Let he whom guilt has riven
no longer hide his head,
for he will be forgiven
if he by faith is led.

And now it's almost morning
to Bethlehem make your way,
to find salvation's dawning
that, after many a day,
since man first lost through sinning
God's own beloved Son,
as told from the beginning,
to share your life has come.

Though many nights may darken
our guilt and suffering,
the star of heavenly pardon
now brightens everything.
Enlightened by his shining,
no more in darkness go,
for God's fair face inclining
salvation will bestow.

God chose to dwell in darkness,
to fill it with his light.
His judgement knows no harshness,
with love does he requite.
For he who formed creation
will not forsake his own.
Who trusts in Christ's salvation
escapes the sinner's doom.

Jochen Klepper

The eternal Word was born, here and this day.
And where was that? Where thou thyself didst
stray.

Though heaven sink down, the earth to fructify,
when will the earth rise up to meet the sky?

Were Christ a thousand times in Bethlehem born
and not in thee, thou wouldst remain forlorn.

So open wide thy heart and let God in,
thou shouldst his kingdom be and he thy king.

When God begot his first-born Son on earth,
he called us to assist the wondrous birth.

What good is Mary's greeting, Gabriel,
if thou be not my messenger as well?

Angelus Silesius
(1624–1677)

All praises to thee, Christ our Lord,
that thou wast born a human child,
born of a maiden undefiled
whom angel hosts sing and applaud.

The eternal Father's only child,
he who is everlasting good,
clothed in our flesh and our poor blood,
lives in a stable bleak and wild.

The world could not contain in space
him who, confined in Mary's womb,
has now become a little one,
yet holds the world in his embrace.

Eternal glory shines so bright
and so transforms this world of sin,
it shines in midnight dark and dim
and makes us children of the light.

So poor on earth is his estate
that he might pity our distress
and make us rich in heavenly grace
and equal to the angels' state.

All this for us he freely bore
to show his love for humankind.
All Christendom rejoice in mind
and thank our Saviour evermore!

Martin Luther (1483–1546)

What is Christmas?

It is the most interesting story
that has ever been told

*Charles Péguy
(1873–1914)*

Our Redeemer was born today,
so we must celebrate with festive joy.
We cannot be sad today
because it is the Lord's birthday.
The saint rejoices
because he is close
to the victor's palm
and the sinner is glad
because forgiveness
will soon be his.
The pagan can breathe in peace
because he is called to life.

Leo the Great
(Pope, d. 461)

When we look for you within ourselves,
when we worship you in the form of bread,
when we speak with you, the Lord of the world,
when we thank you for our lives,
when we offer you the pain caused by
our mistakes
and ask you to help us –
we always see you as an adult.
But every year at Christmas,
you reveal yourself to us
as a child born in a crib.
We stand in silent amazement
and do not know what to ask.
We do not want to be a nuisance to you,
for, although you are omnipotent,
you show yourself as a child.

In silent adoration we stand before the mystery,
like Mary when the shepherds came
and told her what they had seen and heard:
'She kept all these things,
pondering them in her heart'.

Christmas:
Again and again the Child appears to us
as one of the most profound mysteries of faith
and as the first sign of that love for us
that will be made manifest
in the fullness of God's mercy and omnipotence.

Chiara Lubich (b.1920)

Child, dear child,
help me to discover
even in the most earnest
and the most severe people
the child asleep in their hearts.

★ ★ ★

Mary, full of grace,
your son was born
but you continue to be pregnant,
full of grace,
full of God.

★ ★ ★

In the vigil
that we keep again tonight
to celebrate
the Word's becoming human,
there is the prayer
that has proved to be
the most valuable of all —
silence.

*Dom Helder Camara
(b.1909)*

Christ,
we thank you
that we are able to achieve something,
even though we are so fragile.

We praise you, Jesus Christ,
because you know
how helpless we are
and yet continue to come
to sing in us
the joyful song
of unshakable trust.

Brother Roger
(Taizé)

Like a mother rejoicing over her new born
   baby,
like a child rejoicing over his little brother,
like a bride rejoicing over her bridegroom –
the Church rejoices over Christ,
who brings fulfilment to everyone.
The Church sings with joy on this holy night
because the Son of God was born.
He is our life.
He knows our poverty and our sadness
and our hopes and desires.

Carlo Maria Martini
(Archbishop of Milan, b.1927)

In the crib, Jesus radiates
what the world so much needs today –
gentleness, tenderness, light and hope.

Gentleness – as the answer to all violence.
Tenderness – as the answer to the lack of
    goodness,
benevolence and love of our brothers and sisters
(even among those who call themselves
Christians).
Light – as the answer to the shadows that
    darken
the present time.
Hope – as the answer to those who feel
    abandoned
or who find no meaning in their lives.

Little Sister Magdeleine of Jesus
(Founder of the Little Sisters of Jesus,
1898–1989)

Christmas means:
He has come.
He has made the night clear.
He has made the night of our darkness,
the night of our lack of understanding,
the cruel night
of our fears
and our hopelessness
into Christmas, the holy night.

In the Word made flesh,
God has sent his last Word,
his most profound Word,
his most beautiful Word
into the world.
And that Word means:
I love you,
world and humanity.
Light the candles!
They have more right here
than darkness.

Karl Rahner

. . . I am very troubled about you. How
are you going to spend Christmas this year?
Father died at Christmas in 1897 and God
called Mother, our dear Mother, to be with
him only two years ago – also at Christmas.
And now, this year, I, your brother, who have
only ever loved and respected you, have been
taken from you.

I shall celebrate Christmas this year within
a very clearly defined framework – that of this
prison cell. I have never knelt in front of the
crib in such poverty as I am doing this year.
Everything has been taken away from me – my
home, my honour, even my life itself. So I am
kneeling in front of the crib of the one who
had nothing, who had nowhere to lay his head,
who was condemned to death as the friend of
his people and who poured out his blood as a
libation for the salvation of his own people and
of the whole world.

The gifts that I bring this Christmas to
the crib are hunger, cold, loneliness and
forsakenness. The only finery I am wearing are
these shackles. So all that I can give is my life
itself, which has always been in the service of
the Christmas king, and I give it to him who has
redeemed me with his precious blood. I wash

away everything that has become guilt and sin in me with rich tears of repentance and come as a pilgrim to the crib in an attitude of sorrow, hoping to celebrate Christmas with God's grace more deeply in my heart and mind than I have ever celebrated it in the past. This time, I will not be distracted by any Christmas food or presents or by any candles or decorations or by a Christmas tree. I will not even be able to celebrate or go to Mass. But the Child Jesus in the Eucharist will be present with me as the wonderful reality of Christmas, illuminating my life with eternal light and filling me with the warm glow of his love.

I will read the breviary, slowly, intensely and prayerfully, savouring the sweetness of every word, and I will very quietly sing the office of Prime to myself. I will also pray the Our Father and Hail Mary with the rosary and I will read Holy Scripture. In this way, I hope, I will share in the peace of Christ and his grace. I am not at all bitter. I can bear everything patiently – with the patience that only Christ can give.

Father Alfons Maria Wachsmann,
who was condemned to death on 21 February 1944
in Brandenburg-Görden,
to his sister Maria.

The world has continued on its course, but it has become the ship of God that no storm can overturn and no current can deflect. Life has continued to obey its laws and to respond to its tensions, but God has subjected himself to those tensions and has fitted himself into them. He now shares them with us and has in this way raised what the whole of humanity is capable of being and doing to a higher level.

We are no longer alone as human beings. We have never been able to live happily and healthily simply on the basis of monologue. It is only in dialogue that we can live sound, full and authentic lives. Every movement towards monologue is evil. But the existence of tensions in God's being and in his burdens is now calling us to share in dialogue with him and that is his way of finally and forever overcoming the most terrible of human illnesses – loneliness. There is now no night that is without light. There is no prison cell without some authentic conversation. There is no lonely mountain path or dangerous descent into the abyss without someone to accompany and lead us.

God is with us. That was his promise and we have wept and beseeched him. And that promise has become a reality in our lives, in quite a different way from what we expected, a much fuller and a much simpler reality than we had thought it would be.

We should not try to avoid God's burdens. They are the way to his blessing. If we continue faithfully to follow the hard way, bearing God's burdens, we shall discover the inner source of reality and the world will reveal itself as being not silent in a sense that is quite different from what we had imagined. The silver threads of the divine mystery of all reality will begin to gleam and sing aloud for us. Those burdens will become a blessing for us, as soon as we recognize them and bear them as God's burdens.

God became human. We did not become God. The human dispensation continues and it must continue. But it is consecrated. And we have become more. We have also been strengthened. Let us trust our life, then, because this night has brought us light. Let us trust life, because we do not live it alone. God lives it with us.

Alfred Delp SJ
(condemned to death in Plötzensee on 2 February 1945)

The true meaning of Christmas
is not to be found exclusively
in the love of hearth and home,
the happiness of children
or the family gathering.
It can also be celebrated
by those who are lonely,
who are separated from their family
or who simply have no family.
Christmas is not just the feast
of those who have something to give –
it is also the feast
of those who have nothing to give
or no one to give to.
It is not only a family feast –
it is also the feast
of those who are alone.

Romano Guardini
(1885–1968)

The Redeemer who was born in Bethlehem
is not a distant and anonymous God.
He is the 'God with us'
who has counted every hair on our heads.
He accompanies each one of us
throughout our lives
and he has accompanied all of us
throughout the whole of our history.
He is looking for inner fellowship with us.

Patriarch Athenagoras
(1886–1972)

What is the real meaning of our giving at Christmas? Christmas presents are not given universally by every nation and culture in the world. Why is it, then, that, unlike other people, we have, since time immemorial, made Christmas the feast of giving? Many different answers could be given to this question by those who specialize in social history or the philosophy of religion, many of them very helpful and edifying. But I would like to ignore scholarship for the moment and suggest that we just question our own hearts.

We may be poor or we may be well off, but all of us will have spent time before Christmas looking for and buying something to give to those we love. We may have spent hours thinking about an unusual gift for someone. Or we may have wanted to surprise the person who receives our present. It may have cost us more money than we could really afford. And one of the happiest experiences in the world is when we look forward with the eager expectation of a child to a Christmas present or the surprise that we feel – or pretend, with a rather painful smile, to feel – when the parcels lying under the Christmas tree are unwrapped. What is revealed in all this is a deep human longing.

In every one of us, there is hidden, somewhere in the depths of our being, a poet or an artist who is prevented from expressing himself or herself by the everyday tasks. As Baudelaire said, our heart is like a captive albatross on the deck of the ship of life – an awkward, incongruous, ridiculous creature when not in the sky, because it is made for flight and its huge wings prevent it from walking.

We are men and women and we have many very ordinary tasks and duties to do in the hustle and bustle of our lives. On grey days we very often think of them as 'wretched hateful jobs'. But our human experience ought really to be different from this. This hustle and bustle ought to be more loving and touch our hearts more closely, but it only leaves us time and money for those ordinary tasks and duties and for what is strictly necessary. It does not touch our hearts at all, but leaves them poor and empty. Goodness withers away in us and so does love, which can only flourish in a unique situation, when everything is in abundance – in a word, when there is a feast.

What happens in the weeks before Christmas? They are weeks of thinking, planning and preparation. The little girl may begin in secret to knit or sew something for her parents. The young man tries to find out, without asking, what kind of gift will really please the girl he loves. Mother may be using all her ingenuity to conjure up happiness from nothing and father may become a boy again and try to put the old model railway in running order or even make some toys himself. And the children, those people who are still wise and not yet disappointed by life's experiences – they feel safe and happy in the care of their parents. Every parent is, after all, the representative of the infinitely rich Christ child.

This is also where we find the deeper metaphysical meaning of the long established tradition of giving special presents at Christmas, the practice of wanting to give much more than we are able to give or can afford to give. When we go beyond our resources and ability in this way, we become aware that there is something that transcends our ordinary everyday tasks and duties, something that gives us an insight into the nature of the kingdom of God, in which all of us are rich, generous in giving and indeed almost as almighty as God himself.

Every gift is – and here I must use a word which is worn out with use and has often been misused, but which no one, however much he or she uses it, can ever deprive of its glory – a symbol of our love. Every present is like a sacramental, a making visible of an invisible good that goes further than our calculations, has no boundaries and recognizes no frontiers. And however poor we may be, so poor that we have, in the weeks before Christmas, to go past the shop windows and their glorious displays of gifts perhaps with a troubled, hurt and even envious heart, we can still say on Christmas day to those we love: I give you my heart. My heart, my loving heart, is like a carefully locked Christmas present. It contains treasures that have still not been discovered. My love is new and full of surprises. It looks forward to receiving a gift in return. And it is renewed and made young again when it hears the only possible answer: I love you too.

Something even deeper than this may also be expressed when we give presents at Christmas. At Christmas we may give something that is more than just ordinary or simply useful. Or it may be just an ordinary present that we found by chance in a shop months ago and have placed under the Christmas tree ourselves. (I am reminded here of the woollen socks my grandmother used to knit for us as Christmas presents when we were children. They were quite different from ordinary socks – but only because an old silver coin or even a gold sovereign was hidden in them.) But whatever the gift may be and however it is given, it reminds us once again that nothing in our ordinary everyday life can be taken for granted, and that it is the greatest and most mysterious gifts of nature and of God, its creator, that we do in fact take for granted in the hustle and bustle of life.

Hugo Rahner
(1900–1968)

The Word became flesh
the hidden became visible,
the uncreated entered creation
and light shone in the darkness.
Everything else came from this –
the candles, the colours, the gifts,
the good wishes and the carols.
But Christmas is not just that alone.
What this unique Christian feast aims to do
is to give us a deep conviction
and a firm faith in one great truth:
When God came down
from heaven to earth for us
he did so because he loves us.
When someone loves us,
life becomes easier for us
and we can understand everything more clearly.
We can detect that person's hand
behind the shadow of our existence.
We often do not know why,
but we know that person's love
lies behind everything.
Our burdens become lighter
and good experiences become quite joyful.
Life is no longer just a bare outline
because love is in flower behind it,
a child is born
and we are surprised
by unexpected happiness.
We know a loving Father is caring for us.

When we believe in a God who loves us,
everything becomes possible,
even if it seems impossible,
like the apparent impossibility
of peace on our earth.

The almighty one came to us
and because of this
our faith can never be too strong.
We can be sure
that our world is moving
in the direction of unity
and we pray with all our heart
that nations and peoples,
societies and generations,
religions and churches
and people of every generation
will come closer and closer to one another.
This movement towards unity
is something that characterizes
the age we are living in.
Many young people believe in this aim
and are committed to achieving it.
The child whose birth we celebrate today
was no less committed to this dream.
He came into the world
so that we should be one
and he laid down his life
so that this dream should become a reality.

Chiara Lubich (b.1920)

Gloria Deo et pax hominibus – these words are over the new-born Saviour. But they were only reached after Joseph, Mary and the Child had followed the way of countless disappointments, discomforts, adversities and unpleasant experiences. From the human point of view, everything should have been quite different, but the Saviour wanted it to be like this and chose this way. He did so to be an example for us – almost a motto, under which we could give glory to God and bring peace to our fellow people. A motto for us and for me!

My present life is so comfortable and so easy. So I have to stir myself and accept the adversities and unpleasant experiences that my work brings, accept them in imitation of my Saviour, just as Mary and Joseph accepted them in the same spirit.

From the diary of Cardinal Augustin Bea (1881–1968)

The divine child
fulfils the promise.
It is only where he is awaited
that he is received.
Otherwise no child
is born for us tonight.
But where he is accepted
he exceeds every expectation.

Jean-Marie Lustiger
(Archbishop of Paris, b.1926)

Shake off thy Sloth, my drouzy Soul, awake;
　　With Angels sing
　　Unto thy King,
　And pleasant Musick make;
Thy Lute, thy Harp, or els thy Heart-strings take,
And with thy Musick let thy Sense awake.
　See how each one the other calls
　To fix his Ivy on the walls,
　Transplanted there it seems to grow
　As if it rooted were below:
　　Thus He, who is thy King,
　　Makes Winter, Spring.

Shall Houses clad in Summer-Liveries
　　His Praises sing
　　And laud thy King,
　And wilt not thou arise?
Forsake thy Bed, and grow (my Soul) more wise,
Attire thy self in cheerful Liveries:
　Let pleasant Branches still be seen
　Adorning thee, both quick and green;
　And, which with Glory better suits,
　Be laden all the Year with Fruits;
　　Inserted into Him,
　　For ever spring.

Thomas Traherne
(1637–1674)

104

Since Bethlehem, our earth has been changed
for ever.
Since then, it has borne God's glory.

Since then, no power has ever been able
to tear this earth out of God's hands.

Cardinal Alfred Bengsch
(1921–1979)

We desire to be able to welcome Jesus
at Christmas time,,
not in a cold manger of our heart
but in a heart full of love and humility,
in a heart so pure,
so immaculate,
so warm with love for one another.

Mother Teresa of Calcutta
(b.1910)

What is Christmas?
It is living in hope,
holding out the hand of reconciliation,
accepting strangers,
helping one another to do good,
wiping away tears.

Every time love is given,
distress is relieved
and someone is made happy,
God comes down from heaven
and brings us light.
That is Christmas.

A carol from Haiti

We are on the way to you . . .

From the villages and towns,
from the hills and valleys,
with suffering brothers and sisters.
with laughing children.
as builders of peace,
as messengers of justice,
as witnesses to your love,
as members of your Church . . .

. . . we are on the way to you.

When we support the weak,
when we pray for the persecuted,
we are on the way to you.

When we celebrate your presence,
you are with your people.

From a Latin American hymn

Lord,
we pray for the people
who are far from you,
for it is above all for them
that you came into the world
on that day.

Chiara Lubich
(b.1920)

This Christmas I pray
for myself,
for all my sisters and brothers,
for all men and women of good will,
for those who are burdened with cares
and for those who are seeking.

Help us,
so that we may see God's smile
in the face of a child.
Give us a new heart,
so that we may receive the divine child,
understand his message
and bear it in our everyday lives.
Give us the strength
to accompany the Lord
throughout the year ahead
and to follow in his footsteps.

Cardinal Léon-Joseph Suenens
(b.1904)

The star of Bethlehem
is a star in the darkness of night
even today.

Edith Stein
(1891–1942)

Our rich world
has claimed Christmas for itself
and has thrust Jesus outside.

Christmas has become a poetic fantasy,
a friendly atmosphere,
an exchange of gifts,
a symbol of light, stars and carols,
a boom in the sale of luxury goods.
And who thinks of Jesus?

He came to his own home,
but his own people did not receive him.
There was no place for him in the inn –
not even at Christmas.

I would so much like to found a business
that would publicize the real meaning of
    Christmas.
I would like to print the most beautiful cards
and have the most impressive figures made.
I would write poems,
collect old and new carols,
illustrate books for children and grown-ups
and write scripts for films and plays.

It is hurtful to experience the way
people cling to Christmas as a season
but reject the child born at Christmas.
So we must at least let it be seen in our homes
who was born on Christmas day
and let us prepare for him
the best feast we have ever prepared.

Chiara Lubich
(b.1920)

Christmas
is the last word
pronounced over us.
It tells us
that we are loved,
that we are free
and that we are able
to follow the way to God,
that we are new-born
and can begin again our life
and our work of building up society.
This word of hope
lies behind all the greetings
that we send to each other
at Christmas.
It is the true meaning
of all the presents
that we send to each other.
The child who comes to us
is the sign given to us
that God has opened the door
that leads to this way.

Carlo Maria Martini
(Archbishop of Milan, b.1927)

Index of First or Opening Lines

A light has come from Bethlehem (Igino Giordani)   37

All praises to thee, Christ our Lord (Martin Luther)   81

And the Word became flesh (Irenaeus of Lyons)   13

Anyone who has really understood (Karl Barth)   57

Child, dear child (Helder Camara)   85

Christ, we thank you (Brother Roger of Taizé)   86

Christmas, a season of paradox (Charles Wheatley)   43

Christmas. Heaven has opened its gates (Chiara Lubich)   55

Christmas is our feast (Gregory Nazianzen)   76

Christmas is the last word (Carlo Maria Martini)   114

Christmas means (Karl Rahner)   89

Christmas! On that night (Raoul Follereau)   56

Gloria Deo et pax hominibus (Augustin Bea)   102

God became a child (Chiara Lubich)   38

God fulfilled the promises (Odo Casel)   53

God is the Lord (Basil the Great)   63

God, the Lord, has made his mercy known (Francis of Assisi)   68

God's becoming human (Klaus Hemmerle)   44

God's Son became a human being (Alfred Bengsch)   70

God's Son became human (Hildegard of Bingen)   49

Gold, friends, power and honour (Martin Luther)   67

He became a child (Ambrose of Milan)   20

He is simply there (Klaus Hemmerle)   59

How I admire the Lord (Jerome)   31

How much you have loved us (Augustine of Hippo)   39

I am very troubled about you (Alfons Maria Wachsmann)   90

I sing the birth was born to-night (Ben Jonson)   26

I stand here by your manger bed (Paul Gerhardt)   28

If we are to understand (Karl Lehmann)   46

In the beginning was the Word (The Gospel according to John)   11
In the crib, Jesus radiates (Magdeleine of Jesus)   88
In the vigil (Helder Camara)   85
In those days a decree went out (The Gospel according to Luke)   18
Jesus came into the world (René Voillaume)   21
Jesus Christ – God who became human (Julius Angerhausen)   65
Jesus comes back into the world (Werenfried van Straaten)   51
Jesus did not come exclusively (Chiara Lubich)   66
Jesus, what made you so small? (Bernard of Clairvaux)   33
Like a mother rejoicing (Carol Maria Martini)   87
Lord, we pray for the people (Chiara Lubich)   109
Lord! when thou didst thy selfe undresse (Henry Vaughan)   29
Mary, full of grace (Helder Camara)   85
Our Redeemer was born today (Leo the Great)   83
Our rich world (Chiara Lubich)   112
Praise to the holy Trinity (Thomas à Kempis)   75
Shake off thy Sloth, my drouzy Soul, awake (Thomas Traherne)   104
Since Bethlehem, our earth has been changed (Alfred Bengsch)   105
Since this holy night (Odo Casel)   33
The birthday of the Lord (Leo the Great)   54
The divine child (Jean-Marie Lustiger)   103
The drama of human freedom (Carlo Maria Martini)   12
The eternal Word was born, here and this day (Angelus Silesius)   80
The human race was made God's likeness (Andreas Gryphius)   77
The light that shines in the darkness (Carlo Maria Martini)   74
The Lord has sent me (Jean Vanier)   30
The middle of the night (From an old carol)   73
The new world order is this (Zeno of Verona)   52
The night is near its ending (Jochen Klepper)   78
The one who embraces everything (Hilary of Poitiers)   42
The one who has from eternity (Thomas à Kempis)   50
The Redeemer who was born in Bethlehem (Athenagoras)   95
The shepherds sing; and shall I silent be? (George Herbert)   71
The star of Bethlehem (Edith Stein)   111
The true meaning of Christmas (Romano Guardini)   94
The Word became flesh (Klaus Hemmerle)   16
The Word became flesh (Chiara Lubich)   100
The world has continued on its course (Alfred Delp)   93
This Body is not the Cloud (Thomas Traherne)   62

118

This Christmas I pray for myself (Léon-Joseph Suenens)   110
This day our Father did create (Christian Fürchtegott Gellert)   27
This day to you a child is born (Martin Luther)   25
This is the month, and this is the happy morn (John Milton)   34
Thys endris nyghth (Ancient Carol)   22
We are not just promised freedom (Bernard of Clairvaux)   58
We are on the way to you (From a Latin American hymn)   108
We desire to be able to welcome Jesus
    (Mother Teresa of Calcutta)   106
Were my eyes to see you come down (John of the Cross)   39
What is Christmas? (A carol from Haiti)   107
What is Christmas? (Charles Péguy)   82
What is the real meaning of our giving (Hugo Rahner)   96
What suitable response can we make (Hilary of Poitiers)   60
When the King of Kings was born (Gilbert Cesbron)   36
When the time had come (Leo the Great)   45
When we look for you within ourselves (Chiara Lubich)   84
While gentle silence enveloped all things (The Book of Wisdom)   38
Who could doubt the greatness of this event
    (Bernard of Clairvaux)   72
With Jesus a new humanity was born (Carlo Carretto)   40
With the fullness of time he appeared (Augustine of Hippo)   14
You are with us, Emmanuel (Pope John Paul II)   32
You wanted to be God (Augustine of Hippo)   48

Index of Authors

Angerhausen, Julius	64
Ambrose of Milan	20
Athenagoras	95
Augustine of Hippo	14, 39, 48
Barth, Karl	57
Basil the Great	63
Bea, Augustin	102
Bengsch, Alfred	70, 105
·Bernard of Clairvaux	33, 58, 72
Camara, Helder	85
Carol from Haiti, A	107
Carols, ancient and anonymous	22, 73
Carretto, Carlo	40
Casel, Odo	33, 53
Cesbron, Gilbert	36
Delp, Alfred	92
Follereau, Raoul	56
Francis of Assisi	68
Gellert, Christian Fürchtegott	27
Gerhardt, Paul	28
Giordani, Igino	37
Gregory Nazianzen	76
Gryphius, Andreas	77
Guardini, Romano	94
Hemmerle, Klaus	16, 44, 59
Herbert, George	71
Hilary of Poitiers	42, 60
Hildegard of Bingen	49
Irenaeus of Lyons	13
Jerome	31

121

John of the Cross	39
John Paul II, Pope	32
John, The Gospel according to	11
Jonson, Ben	26
Kempis, Thomas à	50, 75
Klepper, Jochen	78
Latin American hymn, From a	108
Lehmann, Karl	46
Leo the Great, Pope	45, 54, 83
Lubich, Chiara	38, 55, 66, 84, 100, 109, 112
Luke, The Gospel according to	18
Lustiger, Jean-Marie	103
Luther, Martin	25, 67, 81
Magdeleine of Jesus	88
Martini, Carlo Maria	12, 74, 87, 114
Milton, John	34
Péguy, Charles	82
Rahner, Hugo	96
Rahner, Karl	89
Roger of Taizé, Brother	86
Silesius, Angelus	80
Stein, Edith	111
Straaten, Werenfried van	51
Suenens, Léon-Joseph	110
Teresa of Calcutta, Mother	106
Traherne, Thomas	62, 104
Vanier, Jean	30
Vaughan, Henry	29
Voillaume, René	21
Wachsmann, Alfons Maria	91
Wheatley, Charles	43
Wisdom, The Book of	38
Zeno of Verona	52